Keeping
Water Clean

by Helen Frost

Consulting Editor: Gail Saunders-Smith, Ph.D.

Reviewer: Carolyn M. Tucker
Water Education Specialist
California Department of Water Resources

Pebble Books

an imprint of Capstone Press
Mankato, Minnesota

Pebble Books are published by Capstone Press,
1710 Roe Crest Drive, North Mankato, Minnesota 56003.
www.capstonepub.com

Printed in the United States of America in North Mankato, Minnesota.
072012
006848R

Library of Congress Cataloging-in-Publication Data
Frost, Helen, 1949–
    Keeping water clean/by Helen Frost.
    p. cm.—(Water)
    Summary: Simple text and photographs describe water pollution, how it
spreads, and its effects.
    ISBN-13: 978-0-7368-0408-0 (hardcover)
    ISBN-10: 0-7368-0408-0 (hardcover)
    ISBN-13: 978-0-7368-4877-0 (softcover pbk.)
    ISBN-10: 0-7368-4877-0 (softcover pbk.)
    1. Water—Pollution—Juvenile literature. [1. Water—Pollution. 2. Pollution.] I.
Title. II. Series.
    TD422.F76 2000
    363.739′4—dc21   99-19590

Note to Parents and Teachers

The Water series supports national science standards for
understanding the properties of water. This book describes and
illustrates ways people can keep water clean. The photographs
support early readers in understanding the text. The repetition of
words and phrases helps early readers learn new words. This book
also introduces early readers to subject-specific vocabulary words,
which are defined in the Words to Know section. Early readers may
need assistance to read some words and to use the Table of
Contents, Words to Know, Read More, Internet Sites, and
Index/Word List sections of the book.

Table of Contents

All living things need clean water to stay alive.

Clean water keeps people, plants, and animals healthy.

Sometimes people pollute water. Polluted water can hurt people, plants, and animals.

Everyone can keep water clean. People can pick up trash from lakes, rivers, and oceans.

12

Farmers can keep water clean. They can use fertilizers that do not pollute the water.

NOTICE
DO NOT
DUMP CHEMICALS
DOWN THIS DRAIN

Factory workers can keep water clean. They can keep chemicals out of the water.

City workers can keep water clean. They can clean the water that people have used.

18

Some groups help keep water clean. They teach people how to take care of water.

Water on the earth is always moving. Keeping water clean can help people everywhere.

Words to Know

factory—a building where products are made in large numbers; factories often use machines and chemicals to make products.

fertilizer—matter that is put on land to make the soil richer and to help crops grow; animal manure and chemical mixtures are types of fertilizers.

healthy—fit and well; clean water keeps people, plants, and animals healthy.

pollute—to make something dirty or unsafe; polluted water can hurt people, plants, and animals.

Read More

Frost, Helen. *We Need Water.* Water. Mankato, Minn.: Pebble Books, 2000.

Hooper, Meredith. *The Drop in My Drink: The Story of Water on Our Planet.* New York: Viking, 1998.

McLeish, Ewan. *Keeping Water Clean.* Protecting Our Planet. Austin, Texas: Raintree Steck-Vaughn, 1998.

Internet Sites

FactHound offers a safe, fun way to find Internet sites related to this book. All of the sites on FactHound have been researched by our staff.

Here's how:

1. Visit *www.facthound.com*

2. Type in this special code **0736804080** for age-appropriate sites. Or enter a search word related to this book for a more general search.

3. Click on the **Fetch It** button.

FactHound will fetch the best sites for you!

Index/Word List

Word Count: 117
Early-Intervention Level: 16

Editorial Credits
Mari C. Schuh, editor; Timothy Halldin, cover designer; Linda Clavel, illustrator;
    Kimberly Danger, photo researcher

Photo Credits
American Water Works Assocation, 18
David F. Clobes, cover, 10, 14, 16
Index Stock Imagery/Exon Photography, 8
International Stock/Steve Lucas, 4
Jack Glisson, 6
Photo Network/Paul Thompson, 1
Photri-Microstock/Fotopic, 20 (top); Lani Howe, 20 (bottom)
Wildlands Conservancy/T.L. Gettings, 12